Little Pebble™

Festivals in Different Cultures

Diwali

by Lisa J. Amstutz

raintree
a Capstone company — publishers for children

Raintree is an imprint of Capstone Global Library Limited, a company incorporated in England and Wales having its registered office at 264 Banbury Road, Oxford, OX2 7DY – Registered company number: 6695582

www.raintree.co.uk
myorders@raintree.co.uk

Edited by Jill Kalz
Designed by Julie Peters
Picture research by Pam Mitsakos
Production by Steve Walker

Printed and bound in China

ISBN 978 1 4747 3793 7
20 19 18 17 16
10 9 8 7 6 5 4 3 2 1

British Library Cataloguing in Publication Data
A full catalogue record for this book is available from the British Library.

Acknowledgements
We would like to thank the following for permission to reproduce photographs: Getty Images: Hemant Mehta, 13; iStockphoto: Hasilyus, 21; Shutterstock: Dipak Shelare, 7, India Picture, 9, 17, 19, indianstockimages, cover, jamesteohart, 1, 22, 24, back cover, phive, 16, Shiny Designer, 3, Sirin_bird, design element, stocksolutions, 15, szefei, 14, TheFinalMiracle, 5; Thinkstock: WebSubstance, 11

Every effort has been made to contact copyright holders of material reproduced in this book. Any omissions will be rectified in subsequent printings if notice is given to the publisher.

All the Internet addresses (URLs) given in this book were valid at the time of going to press. However, due to the dynamic nature of the Internet, some addresses may have changed, or sites may have changed or ceased to exist since publication. While the author and publisher regret any inconvenience this may cause readers, no responsibility for any such changes can be accepted by either the author or the publisher.

Contents

What is Diwali?

Look at all the lights!

Diwali is here!

Diwali is in October or November. This holiday lasts five days.

It is a time to pray
and give thanks.

Getting ready

People clean their homes.
They buy new clothes. They
paint their hands and feet.

Diwali begins

Some people give gifts.

They share sweets.

Families have a feast.

They talk and have fun.

Diyas glow. They welcome the Gods. They show that good wins over evil.

See the pretty art?

Rangoli is made

of sand, rice or flowers.

People put it by the door.

Pop! Boom! Fireworks light the sky. Happy Diwali!

Glossary

Diwali Hindu holiday; Hindus follow the religion of Hinduism

diya oil lamp made from clay

feast large, fancy meal for a lot of people on a special occasion

fireworks rockets that make loud noises and colourful lights when they explode

pray speak to God and give thanks

rangoli patterns made on the floor with coloured sand, rice or flowers

Read more

Diwali (Holidays and Festivals), Nancy Dickman (Heinemann Library, 2011)

A Story of Diwali: The Festival of Light, Pippa Howard (PJ Books, 2012)

Happy Diwali: The Festival of Light, Joyce Bentley (Hachette Children's Group, 2016)

Websites

ww.activityvillage.co.uk/diwali
Learn about Diwali and how it's celebrated.
Play games, enjoy crafts and read stories all about Diwali!

www.diwalifestival.org
Learn about Diwali and what it means to the people that celebrate it.

Comprehension questions

1. Name three things people may do during Diwali.

2. Diyas do two important things. What are they?

Index